BOOK CHARGING CARD

333.75

Accession No. _____ Call No. TOM

Author _Tompkins, Terry_

Title _Ravaged Temperate Forests_

Date Returned

333.75 TOM
Tompkins, Terry
Ravaged Temperate Forests

Ravaged TEMPERATE FORESTS

BY TERRY TOMPKINS

ENVIRONMENT ALERT!

Gareth Stevens Publishing
MILWAUKEE

For a free color catalog describing Gareth Stevens's list of high-quality books, call 1-800-341-3569 (USA) or 1-800-461-9120 (Canada).

ISBN 0-8368-0728-6

A Gareth Stevens Publishing edition

Edited and designed by The Creative Spark of
San Clemente, California, for
Gareth Stevens Publishing
1555 North RiverCenter Drive, Suite 201
Milwaukee, Wisconsin 53212, USA

Picture Credits
Frederick Atwood, pp. 12 (lower), 12-13, 14, 18, 22; Nate Bacon, © 1993, pp. 23, 25; Gary Bublitz/Dembinsky Photo Assoc., © 1993, p. 27 (upper); Francis Caldwell/ Affordable Photo Stock, © 1993, pp. 20-21; Sharon Cummings/Dembinsky Photo Assoc., © 1991, p. 5; Dembinsky Photo Assoc., p. 26; Marvin L. Dembinsky, Jr./Dembinsky Photo Assoc., © 1991, p. 11(lower left inset), © 1992, p. 17 (right); Howard Garrett/ Dembinsky Photo Assoc., © 1993, p. 9; James C. Godwin, © 1993, p. 15; Ron Goulet/ Dembinsky Photo Assoc., © 1993, p. 17 (left); Anthony Mercieca/Dembinsky Photo Assoc., © 1992, front cover (inset); Skip Moody/Dembinsky Photo Assoc., © 1991, p. 11; Sandra Nykerk/Dembinsky Photo Assoc., © 1992, p. 16; Jonathan Perry, front & back cover, pp. 2-3, 5(lower left), 6-7, 7 (right center & lower right), 10-11, 26-27; Carl R. Sams, II/ Dembinsky Photo Assoc. © 1993, p. 7 (upper right), © 1992, p.8, © 1993, p. 11 (right inset), © 1993, p. 19 (lower); Randy Ury, © 1992, p.24. Illus. p. 25 adapted from Margaret B. Davis and Catherine Zabinsky © 1992.

Project editor: Patricia Lantier-Sampon
Series design: Laurie Shock
Book design: Mary Francis-DeMarois
Editorial coordinator and photo research: Elayne Roberts
Editorial consultant: Gregory Lee
Art direction: Elayne Roberts
Illustrations: Teri Rider

Printed in the United States of America
1 2 3 4 5 6 7 8 9 98 97 96 95 94 93

At this time, Gareth Stevens, Inc., does not use 100 percent recycled paper, although the paper used in our books does contain about 30 percent recycled fiber. This decision was made after a careful study of current recycling procedures revealed their dubious environmental benefits. We will continue to explore recycling options.

Production Director   President

CONTENTS

Words that appear in the glossary are printed in **boldface** type the
first time they appear in the text.

THE FOREST COMMUNITY

Many people are concerned today about the world's tropical forests because they are rapidly disappearing. However, humans have had a long and often destructive relationship with another type of forest: the **temperate** forest. Most temperate forests are found in Europe, Asia, and North America, in areas where temperatures fall below freezing for part of the year.

Forests are often referred to by their most common kinds of trees, such as oak-hickory or longleaf pine. But forests are communities with many kinds of living things. Trees, shrubs, and animals share this physical environment. Whenever this environment is disturbed, the impact on all of its species can be devastating.

Forests cover much less of the Earth now than they did before the rise of agriculture. Most forest today is called "second-growth forest." This means that today's forest has regrown in an area where the original, or "old-growth forest," was removed by human hands. Most of the original temperate forest left today is called **boreal** forest. A boreal forest has poor soil and small trees that are unproductive for either farming or lumber.

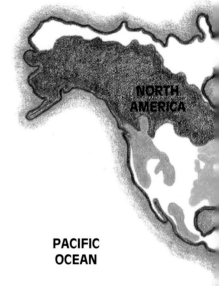

PACIFIC
OCEAN

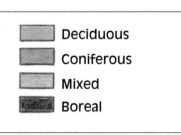

Deciduous
Coniferous
Mixed
Boreal

This is a distribution of large areas of temperate forests. While the majority of temperate forests occur in the areas indicated, smaller patches are scattered across all continents except Antarctica.

Opposite, left: In addition to providing a serene place to walk, the community of this mixed forest interior protects streams from becoming rivers of eroded soil.
Opposite, right: While the boreal forest in many areas stretches on for mile after flat mile, in some places, like Russia and Alaska, the forest combines with mountains to form beautiful vistas.

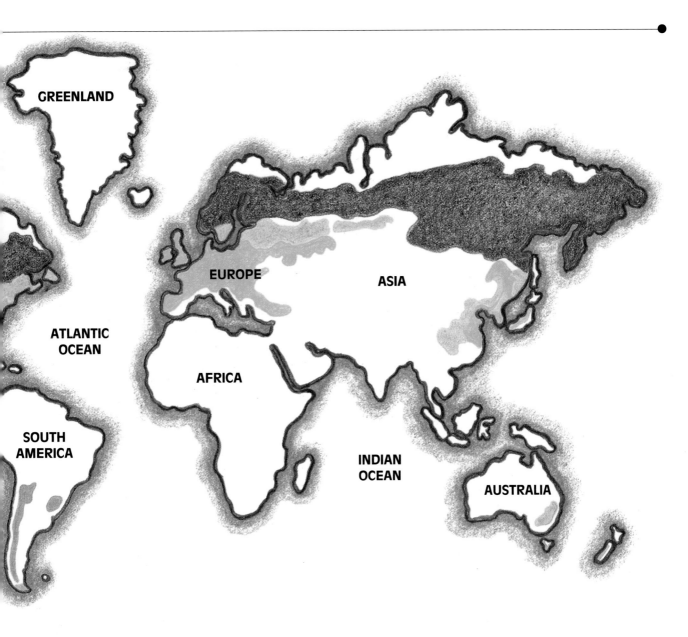

GREENLAND

EUROPE

ASIA

ATLANTIC
OCEAN

AFRICA

SOUTH
AMERICA

INDIAN
OCEAN

AUSTRALIA

Forest Types

Boreal forest is found in the northern areas of the globe, where winters last eight to ten months. It is made up mostly of needle-leaf evergreen trees such as spruce and balsam fir, and forms a kind of belt around the Earth.

To the south of the boreal forests in the eastern United States, western Europe, and eastern China, are the temperate **deciduous** forests. Deciduous forests have broad-leaved trees, such as maple and oak, which stop growing and drop their leaves during the five- to six-month winter. During the warm season, they grow green and lush from the 20 or more inches (50.8 centimeters) of rain they receive. These forests possess a rich layer of soil formed from the broken-down remains of plants.

In western North America, there are temperate **coniferous** forests made up of needle-leaf species such as the Douglas fir, western hemlock, and pine. These trees do well in this warm yet dry region.

Between the boreal forests and the deciduous forests there are often broad bands of mixed forests where both needle-leaf and deciduous trees occur.

Right: Here is the edge of a mixed forest of spruce, birch, and aspen. Opposite, top: This view of mixed spruce and hardwood forest is home to many animal species which either hibernate or migrate south in the winter. Opposite, center: This view shows a mature deciduous forest undergoing fall color change. Opposite, bottom: A view of a second-growth coniferous forest after a fresh snowfall.

FACT FILE
Fire in the Forest

Opposite: A cow elk rests amidst the scarred trunks of pine trees following the Yellowstone Park fire. Fire is one way nature maintains healthy forests.

While people have been told for years about how bad forest fires are, scientists now know that fire is an important part of life in many forests. In some forests, such as the longleaf pine forest of southeastern North America and the jack pine forest in the northern Great Lakes region, fire is necessary for both health and growth. Pine trees need fire to clear away other tree species that compete with them. Fire also helps to open pine cones and release their seeds into the fertile soil. When forests are prevented from having small, cool fires, dry tinder builds up. The risk of having a large, hot fire that kills old trees and destroys pine cones then becomes great. One such large fire occurred in Yellowstone National Park in 1988.

Below: Even after a devastating fire, the forest of Yellowstone Park begins to recover.

Life in a Forest

Within forests, different community members play different roles. For example, the **producer** role—that of turning sunlight into new plant material—is mostly filled by trees, along with some shrubs and **nonwoody** plants.

Producers are continually attacked by **consumers** like insects. Thousands of insect species live in the branches and leaves above the forest, known as the **canopy**. Larger animals like rabbits and deer that eat leaves at ground level are consumers, too. Consumers of plant materials are in turn eaten by **carnivores** such as salamanders, birds, foxes, and wolves.

The group that gets the last turn at the food made by plants is the **decomposers**. This group of organisms lives mostly on the forest floor. Decomposers break down dead plant and animal remains into simple nutrients that growing plants can then use. Examples of this group are earthworms, termites, other insects, and fungi such as mold and mushrooms.

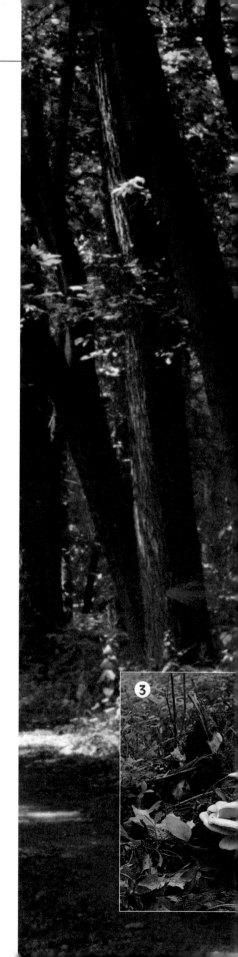

Right: Many species live in and off of these deciduous trees. I.) A blue spotted salamander is discovered searching for a small bug amidst the fall leaf litter. 2.) A deer fulfills its role as consumer by nibbling on tree leaves. 3.) These fungal decomposers are hard at work on the trunk of a fallen tree.

Past Assaults on World Forests

Throughout most of recorded history, the rise of great civilizations has been accompanied by the decline of forests. As large areas of inhabited land began to flourish, the need for fertile soil in which to grow food increased. Wood became necessary to fuel the furnaces of industry, to build the ships of commerce, and to construct great monuments and buildings. To accomplish these things, vast forests were cleared.

Eventually, the loss of trees combined with long-term farming produced poor, eroded soils. Even when areas used for agriculture were abandoned, many forests never grew back. Some historians believe that loss of regional forests and exhaustion of the soil played a large role in the decline of civilizations in Mesopotamia, Greece, Rome, and China.

Both tropical and temperate forests from Haiti to Belize have been marred by clear-cutting.

Current Human Impact

We still lose forest today in tropical areas due to harvesting of trees for fuel and clearing of land for farming. Temperate forest communities, however, are more threatened by clear-cutting. **Clear-cutting** involves cutting down all the woody vegetation and replanting only one or two tree species. Even if these trees grow, the community that was living there has been disrupted. Often, trees planted on a clear-cut do not grow. That is because fires and **herbicides**, chemicals that are applied to clear-cut areas, often kill important species that planted trees need in order to grow.

Opposite: A clear-cut forest is more vulnerable to water erosion, making it harder for the forest to recover and damaging downstream communities.

Below: On hillsides or flatlands, clear-cutting can have an adverse impact on many plant and animal species.

Strip mining and suburban sprawl also lead to loss of forest, while the harm caused by **acid rain** threatens forest communities in both Europe and North America. Acid rain kills trees by attacking their roots.

Another strain on today's forests is the waste of wood by people living in industrialized countries. For example, much wood is wasted in the home construction industry. Overpackaging many products and using new paper rather than recycled paper wastes still more. As a result, the old-growth boreal forests that supply a large share of the world's pulpwood are threatened.

Opposite, left: In forests such as this one, acid rain is causing large areas of coniferous forest to grow sick and die. Opposite, right: Strip mining operations clear vast areas of landscape.

Below: As human populations grow, more and more housing projects like this one will claim forest land, as well as other natural landscapes like grasslands and wetlands.

FACT FILE
Declining Forest Interior Birds

The stillness in the forests of eastern North America has conservationists worried. This stillness is due to the decreased numbers of birds of many species that live in the forest interior. These species, which spend winter in the tropics, seem to be declining for two reasons. First, some appear to be affected by **deforestation** of their winter habitat in the tropics. Second, other birds appear to be unable to adjust to temperate forest **fragmentation**. Fragmentation reduces forest interior and creates more forest edge.

Below: Patches of clear-cut forest not only disrupt bird communities, but can also lead to severe erosion on sloped ground.

Why do some birds dislike the edge of the forest? Many of the declining bird species build their nests either on or near the ground. Animals that eat eggs and nestlings tend to follow forest edges, so nests there are more easily discovered. As a result, forest interior birds either do not build nests near the edge or, if they do, they more often lose their young. In either case, the result is a drop in bird numbers.

Other species in fragmented forests have been hurt by the egg-laying habits of the brown-headed cowbird. This species, which likes open habitat and edge areas, does not build a nest. It prefers to lay its eggs in the nests of other species and trick them into raising its young. Often the other species' young suffer or die because the baby cowbirds get most of the food.

The Kirtland warbler

One bird species that had been severely threatened by the cowbird's behavior was the Kirtland warbler of Michigan. Fortunately, with controlled burns to enhance growth of young jack pines and the removal of cowbirds to reduce their impact, the Kirtland warbler population has begun a slow comeback.

Left: A female cowbird has slipped two of her speckled eggs into the nest of another bird species.

REFORESTATION AND OLD GROWTH PRESERVATION

With little old-growth forest left in temperate regions, it is important that the peoples of the world preserve as much as they can. They should also protect second-growth forest that is more than 100 years old. Since 1900, many forests have been replanted with tree farms that grow only one or two kinds of trees. These farms concentrate on wood production, however, and ignore the rest of the forest community.

One alternative to tree farming is called "new forestry." New forestry attempts to get as much wood as possible out of managed stands of trees, thus lowering the need to cut mature second-growth and old-growth forests. However, unlike tree farming, new forestry tries to increase forest **diversity** by cutting only certain trees instead of all the trees. This improves the long-term health of the forest.

Right: An old-growth coniferous forest in Olympic National Park, Washington.

Increasing the amount of forest and decreasing clear-cutting also helps prevent soil erosion. This reduces the threat of severe floods and helps clean the water many people rely on for living.

People also need to encourage healthy, long-term forest growth to allow trees to continue **photosynthesis**. This process changes airborne carbon dioxide into new plant matter. This may reduce the threat of global warming caused by the recent increase in airborne carbon dioxide.

Opposite: Tree plantations, such as this one in Germany, are used to grow single species, usually for manufacturing purposes.

Below: This reforestation project in Costa Rica will take many years to complete.

FACT FILE
Global Warming

Some scientists study past plant communities by looking at plant parts left in ancient mud. They have found that when global climate has changed—as it did following the last ice age—most plant species were able to follow the climate where they grew best. However, these scientists have also found that different plant species "migrate" at different rates.

This causes concern because many forest communities are weakened by human activity. These communities may not thrive when they must move together to stay healthy because different species shift ranges at different rates. In addition, past shifting took place slowly, when forests were large and unbroken by open spaces.

Because the climate may change due to the gradual warming of the Earth's atmosphere (called *global warming*), species of today's fragmented forests may find that shifting fast enough will be difficult. They may need help in "jumping" the open spaces between today's forest patches. This help can come from people in the form of spreading seeds of species in areas where the new climate is best for them.

The American Chestnut

When Europeans first arrived in the New World, one in every four trees in the eastern forest was an American chestnut. Around 1900, a fungus pest that destroyed chestnut trees in Asia was accidentally introduced into North America. By the end of World War II, the American chestnut was nearly wiped out. Only a few isolated stands and young trees sprouting from old root stock remained. Today, scientists are working to breed a resistant chestnut from the few remaining stands. Other researchers are close to developing a vaccine that will protect the American chestnut much like the polio vaccine protects humans.

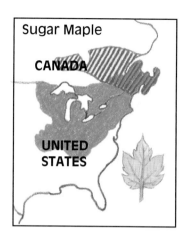

Sugar Maple

CANADA

UNITED STATES

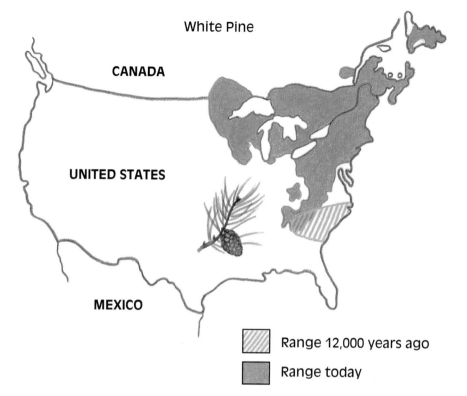

White Pine

CANADA

UNITED STATES

MEXICO

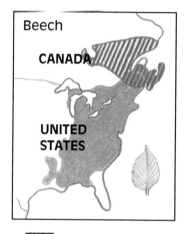

Beech

CANADA

UNITED STATES

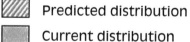

Range 12,000 years ago

Range today

Predicted distribution

Current distribution

The maps above show the predicted change in distribution of two deciduous forest tree species as average global temperatures increase. Both the sugar maple and the beech will shift northward to follow the climate ranges where they grow best.

Right: Foresters determine whether to cut a mature deciduous tree in this second-growth forest.

Efficiency and Recycling Save Trees

The switch to new forestry from tree farming may reduce the rate of wood harvest in coming years. To help make the change, the use of wood will have to be reduced. There are many ways to do this. About one-fourth of the industrial use of wood is for pulp to make paper products. Most of the developed world could improve its recycling programs and increase its use of recycled paper. While Japan recycles 50 percent and Sweden 40 percent of their paper products, the rest of the developed world recycles only one-third or approximately 33 percent.

Below, left: Sawmills consume vast amounts of timber.

Opposite: All communities should recycle whenever possible to help preserve the world's forests.

Below, right: This paper is headed for a recycling mill. The return and reuse of this paper saves many trees.

Most of the remaining wood that is cut is used to make lumber, plywood, and chipboard. These products are used in the building industry, but often wastefully. People need to discourage waste. Fortunately, some builders already instruct their workers on reducing waste.

Engineers need to develop ways to construct safe, strong buildings using less wood. New ways are also needed to reduce waste when raw wood is converted into finished products. As the human population continues to grow, it must learn to use natural resources more efficiently. If this is done, we will leave future generations a healthy planet to cherish and nourish.

RESEARCH ACTIVITIES

1. Listen in the forest.

Springtime is best. Count the different kinds of birds you see. Now count the different kinds of birds you hear. Which number is higher? An adult should be able to help you identify some of the species you see and hear.

2. Look in the forest.

Lie face down on the forest floor. Move aside the upper leaves and twigs, and watch the small, living things you will uncover. Be careful not to disturb them. Count the different kinds of bugs, worms, and other things you see. Are there any white, hairlike, fungal filaments? All these creatures play an important role in breaking down plant matter.

3. Recycle paper.

Have your class at school (or your family at home) save all the paper it uses in a day or a week. Weigh it and talk about ways you may be able to use less. A month later do it again, and see if you have reduced the amount of paper you use.

Things You Can Do to Help

The following activities will help stop the destruction of temperate forests. Try to involve your friends, family, and classmates in your conservation efforts.

1. **Organize a schoolwide wood and paper recycling program.** Write a letter to a community leader telling him or her how you would like the entire community to conserve forests by reducing paper use or recycling more.

2. **List all things you use that are made of wood.** Take good care of these products so you can use them over and over to reduce our need to cut more trees.

3. **Organize a bake sale, car wash, or other fund-raising event with your friends and classmates.** Use the money to join and help support Save America's Forests, 4 Library Court, S.E., Washington, D.C. 20003. This group works to preserve all kinds of forests worldwide.

Places to Write for More Information

The following organizations work to save the environment. When you write to them for more information, be specific about what you want to know and include an envelope with a stamp and your address so they can write back to you.

Children for Old Growth
P.O. Box 1090
Redway, CA 95560

Soil Conservation Service
U.S. Department of
    Agriculture
Washington, DC 20250

Environmental Youth
    Alliance
P.O. Box 34097, Station D
Vancouver, British Columbia
V6J 4M1

More Books to Read

Animal Homes: Forests, by Shirley Greenway (Newington Press)
Ecology: A Practical Introduction with Projects and Activities,
    by Richard Spurgeon (Usborne)
Endangered Forest Animals, by Dave Taylor (Crabtree)
Habitats: Where the Wild Things Live, by Randi Hacker and Jackie Kaufman
    (John Muir Publications)
The Living Forest, by Peter K. Schoonmaker (Enslow Publishers)

Glossary

acid rain — polluted rain or snow that endangers living things.

boreal — cold temperate region of the northern hemisphere.

canopy — the upper layer of leaves in a forest.

carnivore — an animal that eats other animals.

clear-cutting — completely logging a section of forest until there are no trees.

coniferous — a type of woody plant that bears its seeds in cones.

consumer — an animal that eats plants or other animals.

deciduous — a type of woody plant that loses its leaves during winter.

decomposers — species that break down dead material into simple nutrients which plants can use to help them grow.

deforestation — the elimination of forest from a large area.

diversity — a measure of how many kinds of organisms live in an area.

fragmentation — the breaking of habitat into smaller and smaller patches.

habitat — the natural home of a plant or animal species.

herbicide — a toxic chemical designed to kill plants.

nonwoody — plants without wood in the stems.

photosynthesis — a process using sunlight to turn water and carbon dioxide into sugar and oxygen.

producers — plants that are able to change light energy into living tissue.

strip mining — obtaining minerals by digging huge open pits in the ground.

temperate — not extreme; the area of warm summers and cold winters found between the warm tropics and the cold polar regions.

Index